EASY POP MELODIES
FOR CELLO

ISBN 978-1-4803-8437-8

HAL•LEONARD®
CORPORATION
7777 W. BLUEMOUND RD. P.O. BOX 13819 MILWAUKEE, WI 53213

Visit Hal Leonard Online at
www.halleonard.com

ALL MY LOVING

CELLO

Words and Music by JOHN LENNON
and PAUL McCARTNEY

BEAUTY AND THE BEAST

from Walt Disney's BEAUTY AND THE BEAST

CELLO

Lyrics by HOWARD ASHMAN
Music by ALAN MENKEN

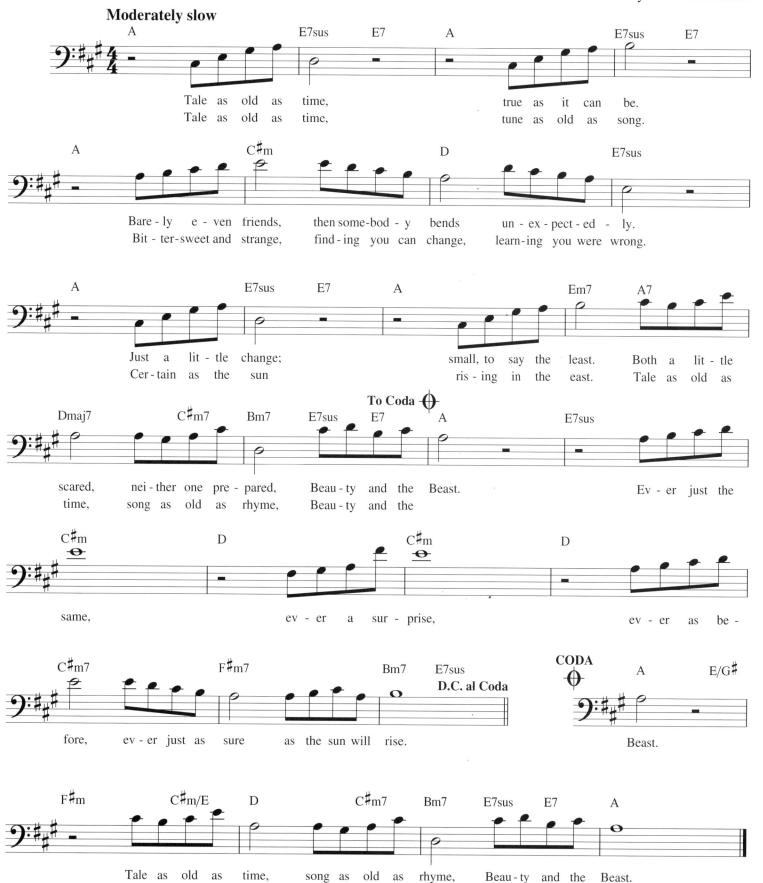

BLOWIN' IN THE WIND

CELLO

Words and Music by
BOB DYLAN

CAN YOU FEEL THE LOVE TONIGHT
from Walt Disney Pictures' THE LION KING

CELLO

Music by ELTON JOHN
Lyrics by TIM RICE

CAN'T HELP FALLING IN LOVE

CELLO

Words and Music by GEORGE DAVID WEISS,
HUGO PERETTI and LUIGI CREATORE

CLOCKS

Words and Music by GUY BERRYMAN,
JON BUCKLAND, WILL CHAMPION
and CHRIS MARTIN

CELLO

DAYDREAM BELIEVER

CELLO

Words and Music by
JOHN STEWART

DON'T KNOW WHY

CELLO

Words and Music by
JESSE HARRIS

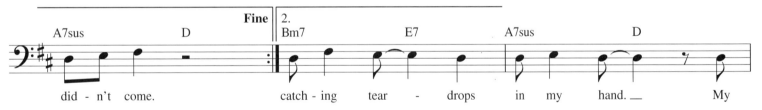

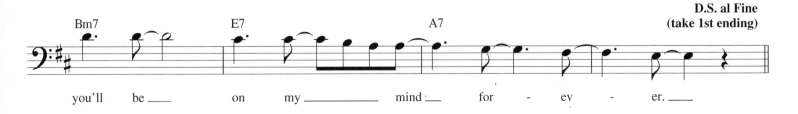

DON'T STOP BELIEVIN'

CELLO

Words and Music by STEVE PERRY,
NEAL SCHON and JONATHAN CAIN

EDELWEISS
from THE SOUND OF MUSIC

CELLO

Lyrics by OSCAR HAMMERSTEIN II
Music by RICHARD RODGERS

EIGHT DAYS A WEEK

CELLO

Words and Music by JOHN LENNON
and PAUL McCARTNEY

Moderately fast

1., 3. Ooh,   I   need your   love,   babe;   guess you   know   it's   true.
2. Love   you   ev - 'ry   day,   girl;   al - ways   on   my   mind.

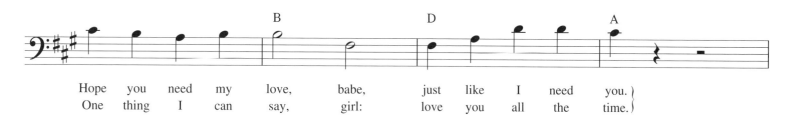

Hope   you   need   my   love,   babe,   just   like   I   need   you.)
One   thing   I   can   say,   babe,   girl: love   you   all   the   time.)

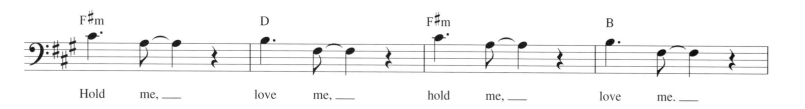

Hold   me, ___   love   me, ___   hold   me, ___   love   me. ___

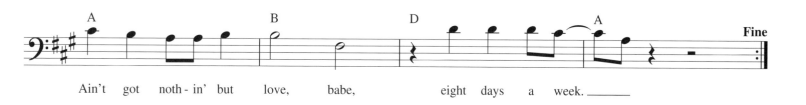

Ain't   got   noth - in'   but   love,   babe,   eight   days   a   week. ___

Eight   days   a   week   I   love _____ you.

Eight   days   a   week   is   not   e - nough   to   show   I   care. ___

EVERY BREATH YOU TAKE

CELLO

Music and Lyrics by
STING

FIREFLIES

CELLO

Words and Music by
ADAM YOUNG

GEORGIA ON MY MIND

CELLO

Words by STUART GORRELL
Music by HOAGY CARMICHAEL

IN MY LIFE

CELLO

Words and Music by JOHN LENNON
and PAUL McCARTNEY

HEY, SOUL SISTER

CELLO

Words and Music by PAT MONAHAN,
ESPEN LIND and AMUND BJORKLAND

Moderately

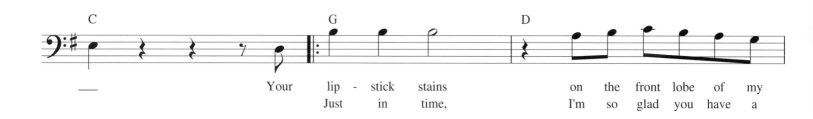

Hey, _____ hey, _____ hey. _____

_____ Your lip - stick stains on the front lobe of my
Just in time, I'm so glad you have a

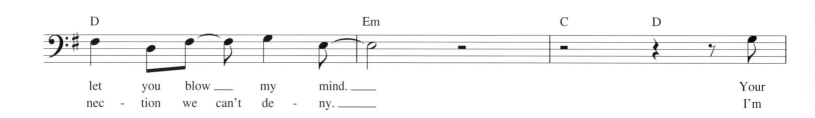

left - side brains. I know I wouldn't for - get ya, and so I went and
one - track mind like me. You gave my life di - rec - tion, a game show love con -

let you blow _____ my mind. _____ Your
nec - tion we can't de - ny. _____ I'm

G   D   Em

sweet moon - beam, the smell of you in ev - 'ry sin - gle dream I dream. _____
so ob - sessed; my heart is bound to beat right out my un - trimmed chest. _____

HOT N COLD

CELLO

Words and Music by KATY PERRY,
MAX MARTIN and LUKASZ GOTTWALD

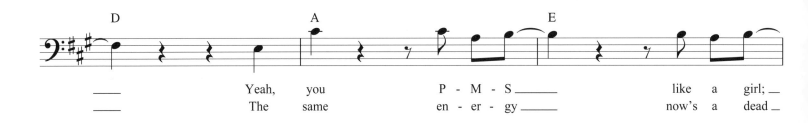

You   change your mind ____ like a girl ____ chang-es clothes. ___
We   used to be ____ just like twins, ___ so in sync. ___

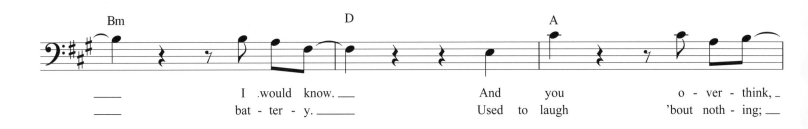

____ Yeah, you   P - M - S ____ like a girl; ___
____ The same   en - er - gy ____ now's a dead ___

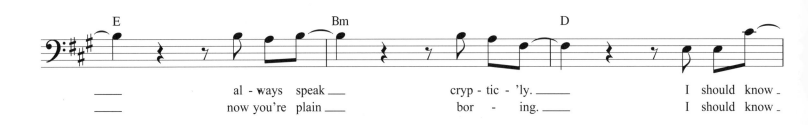

____ I .would know. ___ And you   o - ver - think, ___
____ bat - ter - y. ____ Used to laugh   'bout noth - ing; ___

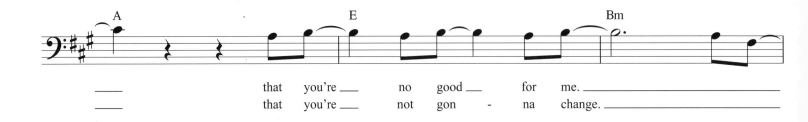

____ al - ways speak ____ cryp - tic - 'ly. ____ I should know ___
____ now you're plain ____ bor - ing. ____ I should know ___

that you're ____ no good ____ for me. _____
that you're ____ not gon - na change. _____

'Cause you're hot ____ then you're cold. You're yes ____ then you're no. You're in ____

____ then you're out. You're up ____ then you're down. You're wrong ____ when it's right. It's black ____

____ and it's white. We fight, ____ we break up. We kiss, ____ we make up. ____

You don't real - ly wan - na stay, no, ____ but you don't real - ly wan - na

go. _____ You're hot ____ then you're cold. You're yes ____ then you're no. You're in ____

____ then you're out. You're up ____ then you're down. ____ ____ then you're down. ____

ISN'T SHE LOVELY

CELLO

Words and Music by
STEVIE WONDER

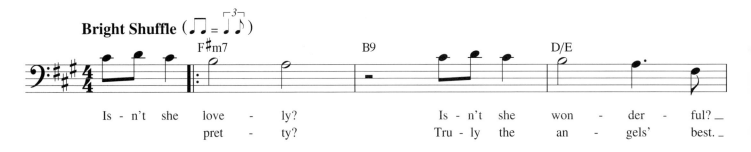

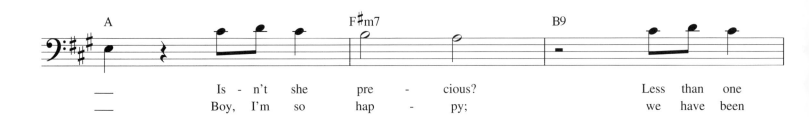

Is - n't she love - ly? Is - n't she won - der - ful?
pret - ty? Tru - ly the an - gels' best. ___

Is - n't she pre - cious? Less than one
Boy, I'm so hap - py; we have been

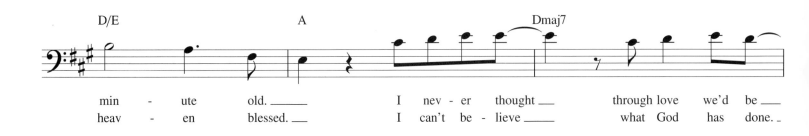

min - ute old. ___ I nev - er thought ___ through love we'd be ___
heav - en blessed. ___ I can't be - lieve ___ what God has done. ___

mak - ing one as love - ly ___ as she. ___ }
Through us He's giv - en life ___ to one. ___ } But is - n't she

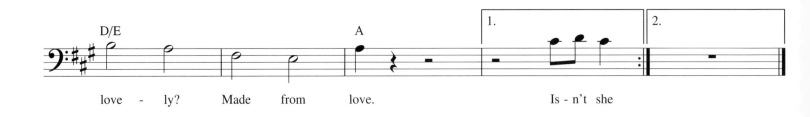

love - ly? Made from love. Is - n't she

THE LETTER

CELLO

Words and Music by
WAYNE CARSON THOMPSON

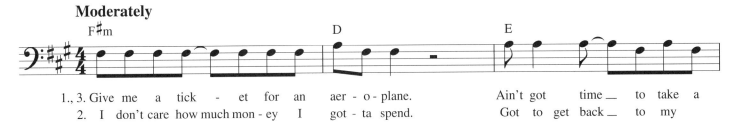

1., 3. Give me a tick - et for an aer - o - plane.
2. I don't care how much mon - ey I got - ta spend.

Ain't got time __ to take a
Got to get back __ to my

fast __ train.
ba - by again.

Lone - ly days are gone; __

I'm a - go - in' home. __ Oh, my

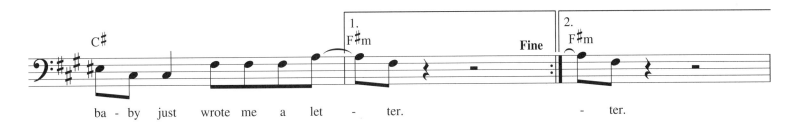

ba - by just wrote me a let - ter.

- ter.

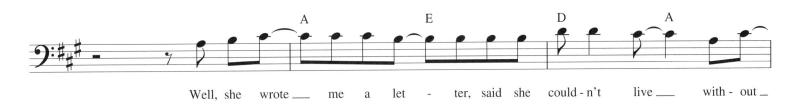

Well, she wrote __ me a let - ter, said she could - n't live __ with - out

__ me no more.

Lis - ten, mis - ter, can't you see I

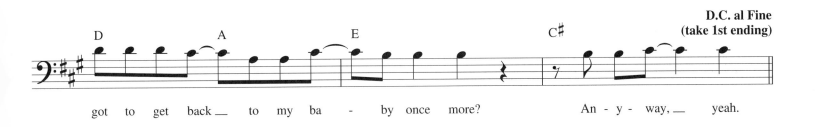

got to get back __ to my ba - by once more?

D.C. al Fine
(take 1st ending)

An - y - way, __ yeah.

LIKE A VIRGIN

CELLO

Words and Music by BILLY STEINBERG
and TOM KELLY

THE LOOK OF LOVE

from CASINO ROYALE

CELLO

Words by HAL DAVID
Music by BURT BACHARACH

LOVE ME TENDER

CELLO

Words and Music by ELVIS PRESLEY
and VERA MATSON

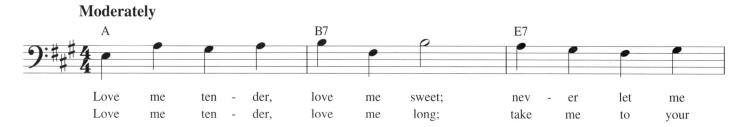

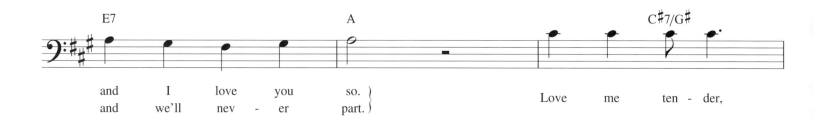

MR. TAMBOURINE MAN

CELLO

Words and Music by
BOB DYLAN

LOVE STORY

CELLO

Words and Music by
TAYLOR SWIFT

Moderately

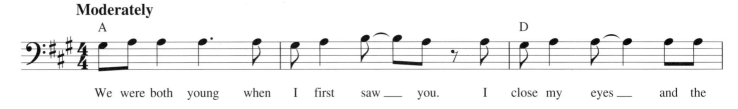

We were both young when I first saw ___ you. I close my eyes ___ and the

flash-back starts. ___ I'm stand-ing there on a bal-co-ny in sum-mer air.

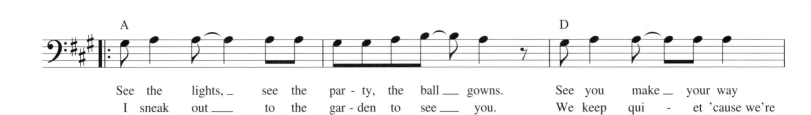

See the lights, ___ see the par - ty, the ball ___ gowns. See you make ___ your way
I sneak out ___ to the gar - den to see ___ you. We keep qui - et 'cause we're

through the crowd ___ and say hel - lo. Lit - tle did I _____ know
dead if they knew, ___ so close your eyes, es - cape this town for a lit - tle while.

that you were Ro - me - o. You were throw-ing peb - bles, and my
'Cause you were Ro - me - o; I was the scar - let let - ter. And my

dad - dy said, "Stay a - way from Ju - li - et." ___ And I was cry - ing on the stair - case,
dad - dy said, "Stay a - way from Ju - li - et." ___ But you were ev - 'ry-thing to me. I was

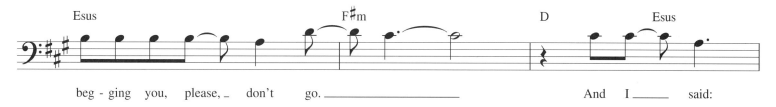

beg - ging you, please, __ don't go. _____ And I ____ said:

Ro - me - o, take me some-where we can be a - lone. I'll be wait - ing.

All there's left to do is run. You'll be the prince and I'll be the prin - cess.

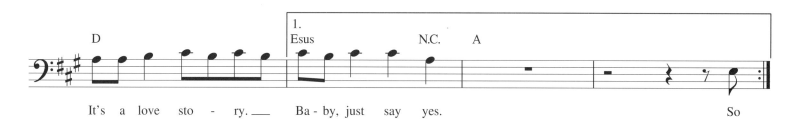

It's a love sto - ry. ___ Ba - by, just say yes. So

Ba - by, just say ____ yes. _____ Oh, ___ oh, oh. __

Oh, ___ oh, oh, _____ oh.

'Cause we were both young when I first saw ___ you. ___

MOON RIVER

from the Paramount Picture BREAKFAST AT TIFFANY'S

CELLO

Words by JOHNNY MERCER
Music by HENRY MANCINI

MORNING HAS BROKEN

CELLO

Words by ELEANOR FARJEON
Music by CAT STEVENS

MY CHERIE AMOUR

CELLO

Words and Music by STEVIE WONDER,
SYLVIA MOY and HENRY COSBY

MY GIRL

Cello

Words and Music by WILLIAM "SMOKEY" ROBINSON
and RONALD WHITE

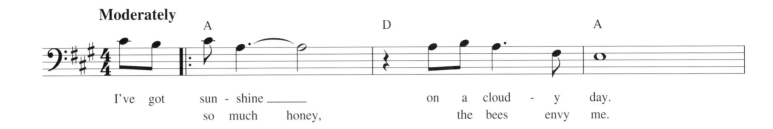

I've got sun - shine _____ on a cloud - y day.
so much honey, the bees envy me.

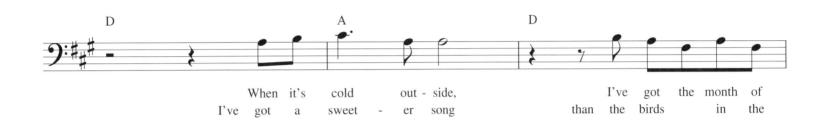

When it's cold out - side, I've got the month of
I've got a sweet - er song than the birds in the

May.)
trees.)   I guess you say, what can make me

feel this way? My girl. (My girl, my girl.) Talk - in' 'bout

my girl. _____ (My girl.) I've got (My girl.)

MY FAVORITE THINGS

from THE SOUND OF MUSIC

CELLO

Lyrics by OSCAR HAMMERSTEIN II
Music by RICHARD RODGERS

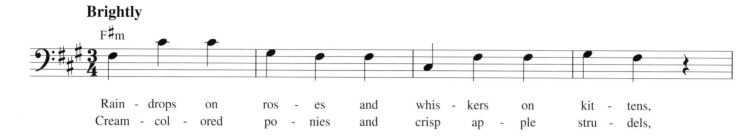

Rain - drops on ros - es and whis - kers on kit - tens,
Cream - col - ored po - nies and crisp ap - ple stru - dels,

bright cop - per ket - tles and warm wool - en mit - tens,
door - bells and sleigh - bells and schnit - zel with noo - dles,

brown pa - per pack - ag - es tied up with strings;
wild geese that fly with the moon on their wings;

these are a few of my fa - vor - ite things.

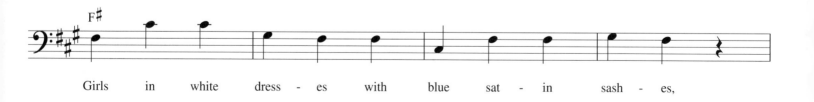

Girls in white dress - es with blue sat - in sash - es,

MY HEART WILL GO ON
(Love Theme from 'Titanic')
from the Paramount and Twentieth Century Fox Motion Picture TITANIC

CELLO

Music by JAMES HORNER
Lyric by WILL JENNINGS

NIGHTS IN WHITE SATIN

CELLO

Words and Music by
JUSTIN HAYWARD

NOWHERE MAN

CELLO

Words and Music by JOHN LENNON
and PAUL McCARTNEY

PUFF THE MAGIC DRAGON

CELLO

Words and Music by LENNY LIPTON
and PETER YARROW

RAINDROPS KEEP FALLIN' ON MY HEAD

from BUTCH CASSIDY AND THE SUNDANCE KID

CELLO

Lyric by HAL DAVID
Music by BURT BACHARACH

SCARBOROUGH FAIR/CANTICLE

CELLO

Arrangement and Original Counter Melody by PAUL SIMON
and ARTHUR GARFUNKEL

SOMEWHERE OUT THERE

from AN AMERICAN TAIL

CELLO

Music by BARRY MANN and JAMES HORNER
Lyric by CYNTHIA WEIL

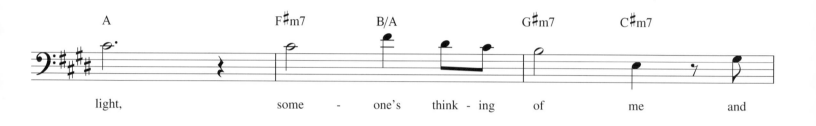

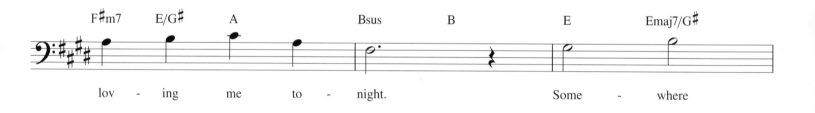

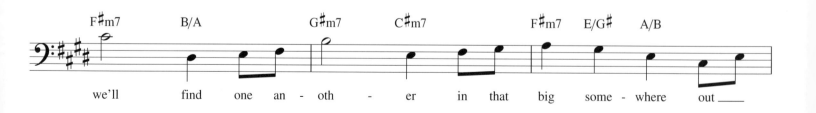

there. And e - ven though I know how ver - y far a - part we are, it

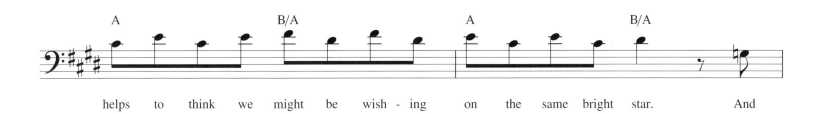

helps to think we might be wish - ing on the same bright star. And

when the night wind starts to sing that lone - some lull - a - by, it

helps to think we're sleep - ing un - der - neath the same big sky.

Some - where out there, if love can see us

through, then we'll be to - geth - er some - where

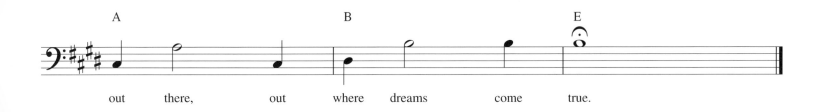

out there, out where dreams come true.

THE SOUND OF MUSIC
from THE SOUND OF MUSIC

CELLO

Lyrics by OSCAR HAMMERSTEIN II
Music by RICHARD RODGERS

Moderately

The hills are a - live with the sound of mu - sic, _____ with

songs they have sung for a thou - sand years. _____ The

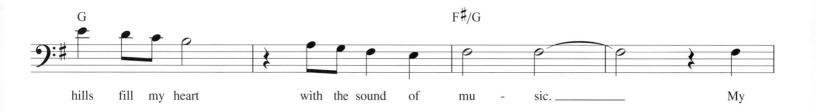

hills fill my heart with the sound of mu - sic. _____ My

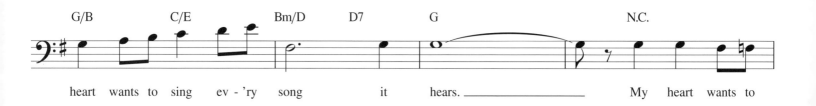

heart wants to sing ev - 'ry song it hears. _____ My heart wants to

beat like the wings of the birds that rise from the lake to the

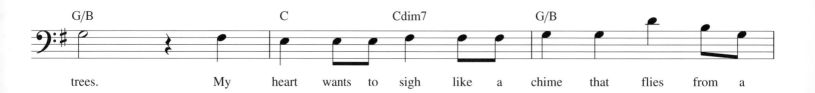

trees. My heart wants to sigh like a chime that flies from a

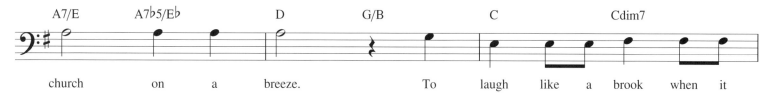

church   on   a   breeze.   To   laugh   like   a   brook   when   it

trips   and   falls   o - ver   stones   in   its   way,   to

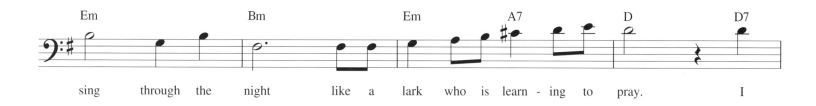

sing   through   the   night   like   a   lark   who   is   learn - ing   to   pray.   I

go   to   the   hills   when   my   heart   is   lone - ly. _____   I

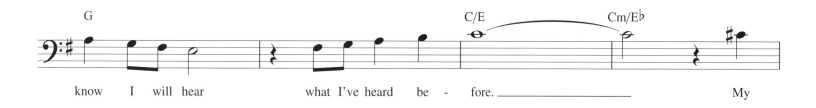

know   I   will   hear   what   I've   heard   be - fore. _____   My

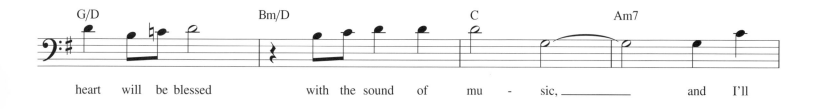

heart   will   be   blessed   with   the   sound   of   mu - sic, _____   and   I'll

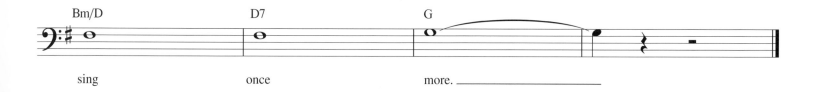

sing   once   more. _____

STRANGERS IN THE NIGHT
adapted from A MAN COULD GET KILLED

Cello

Words by CHARLES SINGLETON and EDDIE SNYDER
Music by BERT KAEMPFERT

SUNSHINE ON MY SHOULDERS

CELLO

Words by JOHN DENVER
Music by JOHN DENVER, MIKE TAYLOR
and DICK KNISS

SWEET CAROLINE

Words and Music by
NEIL DIAMOND

CELLO

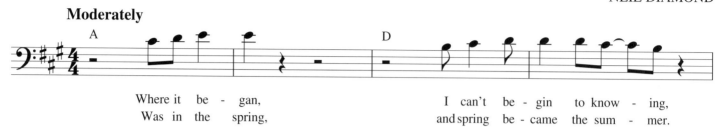

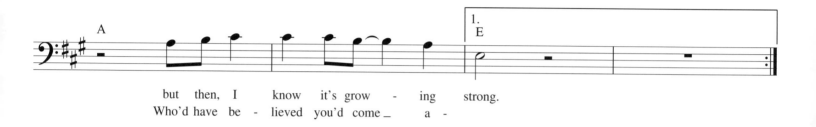

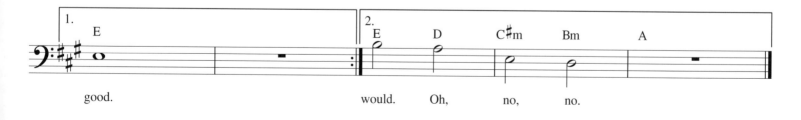

TILL THERE WAS YOU
from Meredith Willson's THE MUSIC MAN

CELLO

By MEREDITH WILLSON

THE TIMES THEY ARE A-CHANGIN'

CELLO

Words and Music by
BOB DYLAN

UNCHAINED MELODY

CELLO

Lyric by HY ZARET
Music by ALEX NORTH

TOMORROW
from The Musical Production ANNIE

CELLO

Lyric by MARTIN CHARNIN
Music by CHARLES STROUSE

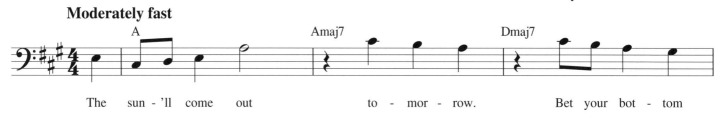

Moderately fast

The sun-'ll come out to - mor - row. Bet your bot - tom

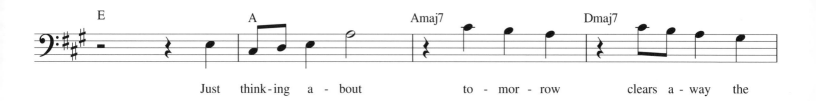

dol - lar that to - mor - row there'll be sun.

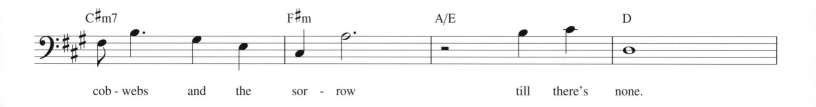

Just think-ing a - bout to - mor - row clears a - way the

cob - webs and the sor - row till there's none.

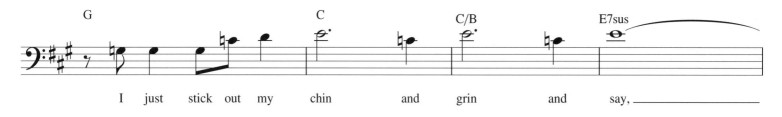

When I'm stuck with a day that's gray and lone - ly,

I just stick out my chin and grin and say, ____

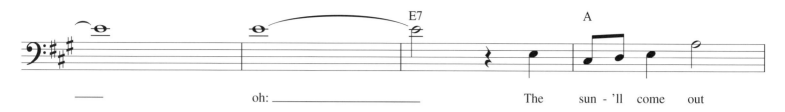

oh: _____ The sun - 'll come out

to - mor - row, so you got - ta hang on till to - mor - row,

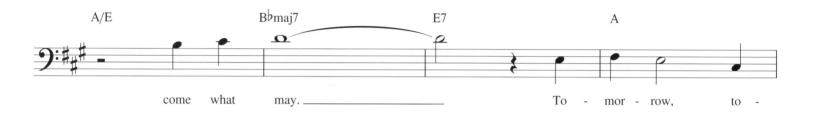

come what may. _____ To - mor - row, to -

mor - row, I love ya, to - mor - row. You're al - ways a

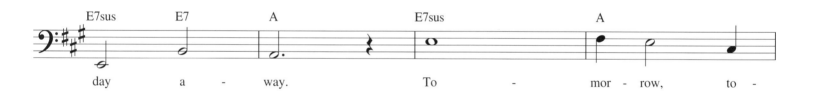

day a - way. To - mor - row, to -

mor - row, I love ya, to - mor - row. You're al - ways a

day _____ a - way! _____

VIVA LA VIDA

Words and Music by GUY BERRYMAN,
JON BUCKLAND, WILL CHAMPION
and CHRIS MARTIN

CELLO

Moderately

I used to rule the world. ___ Seas would rise when I gave the word. ___

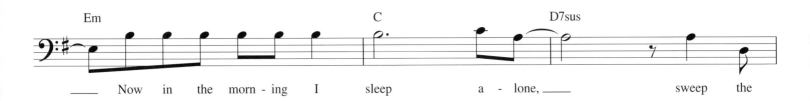

___ Now in the morn-ing I sleep a - lone, ___ sweep the

streets I used to own. _____

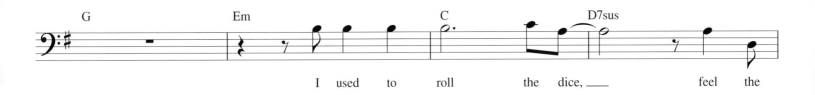

I used to roll the dice, ___ feel the

fear in my en - e - my's eyes, _____ lis - ten as the crowd ___ would sing,

___ "Now the old king is dead; ___ long live the king." One min - ute I

held the key, ___ next the walls were closed on

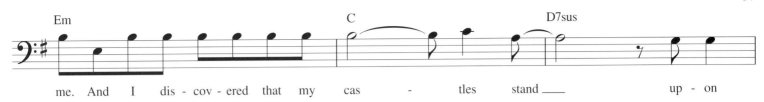

me. And I dis - cov - ered that my cas - tles stand _____ up - on

pil - lars of salt ___ and pil - lars of sand. _____ I hear Je - ru - sa - lem bells ___

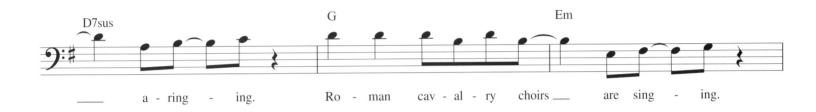

___ a - ring - ing. Ro - man cav - al - ry choirs ___ are sing - ing.

Be my mir - ror, my sword ___ and shield, _____ my mis - sion - ar - ies in a for -

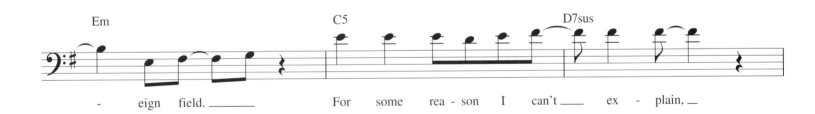

- eign field. _____ For some rea - son I can't ___ ex - plain, _

once you've gone there was nev - er, nev - er an hon - est word, _

____ and that was when I ruled the world. ___

WE ARE THE WORLD

CELLO

Words and Music by LIONEL RICHIE
and MICHAEL JACKSON

WHAT A WONDERFUL WORLD

Words and Music by GEORGE DAVID WEISS
and BOB THIELE

CELLO

WONDERWALL

CELLO

Words and Music by
NOEL GALLAGHER

_____ the lights _ that lead _____ us there _ are blind - ing.

There are man - y things _____ that I _____ would like to say to you, _

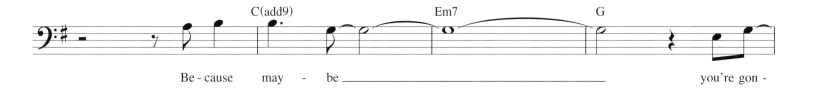

_____ but I don't know how. _____

Be - cause may - be _____ you're gon -

- na be the one that saves me, _____ and

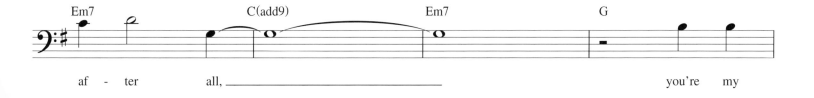

af - ter all, _____ you're my

won - der - wall. _____

YOU ARE THE SUNSHINE OF MY LIFE

CELLO

Words and Music by
STEVIE WONDER

You are the sun - shine of ___ my life. ___
You are the ap - ple of ___ my eye. ___

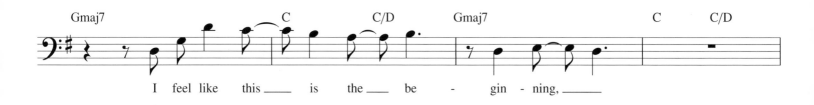

That's why I'll al - ways be ___ a - round. ___
For - ev - er you'll ___ stay in ___ my heart. ___

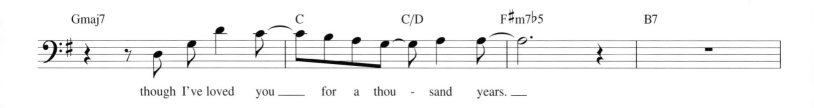

I feel like this ___ is the ___ be - gin - ning, ___

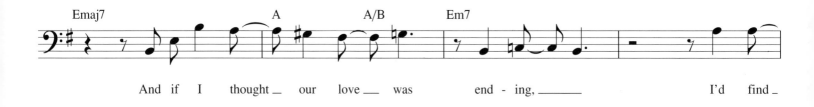

though I've loved you ___ for a thou - sand years. ___

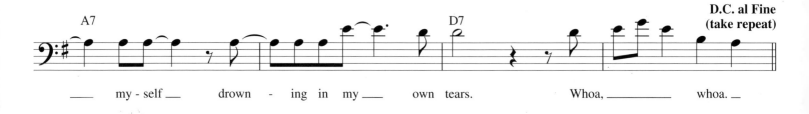

And if I thought ___ our love ___ was end - ing, ___ I'd find ___

___ my - self ___ drown - ing in my ___ own tears. Whoa, ___ whoa. ___

YOU'VE GOT A FRIEND

CELLO

Words and Music by
CAROLE KING

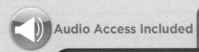

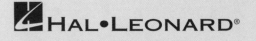